Chatta Manawaka

©2015 All Rights Reserved

ISBN: 978-955-8865-69-9

Computer Typesetting by

Mahamevnawa Buddhist Monastery, Toronto
Markham, Ontario, Canada L6C 1P2
Telephone: 905-927-7117
www.mahamevnawa.ca

Published by

Mahamegha Publishers
Waduwawa, Yatigaloluwa, Polgahawela, Sri Lanka.
Telephone: +94 37 2053300 I 77 3216685
www.mahameghapublishers.com
mahameghapublishers@gmail.com

Chatta Manawaka

*With the guidance and direction of
Most Venerable Kiribathgoda Gnānānanda Thera*

Artwork by Sumathipāla & Jothipāla

A Mahamegha Publication

*Namo Tassa Bhagavato Arahato
Sammā Sambuddhassa!*

*Homage to the Blessed One, the Worthy One,
the Supremely Enlightened One!*

Chatta Manavaka

Dear children, this is a beautiful story about a young boy who lived in India during the times of the Buddha. When you read this story, you will realize the value of taking refuge in the Noble Triple Gem and the importance of virtue. If you can understand what the Noble Triple Gem is and become virtuous by observing the precepts, then the protection you'll gain would be immeasurable.

The boy's name was Chatta Manawaka. He was very talented and wise. He completed his studies quite fast.

There was a custom during that time, to offer gifts to the teacher once a student completes his studies. So one day, Chatta Manavaka too went to meet his teacher to offer the gifts. The road to the teacher's home fell through a wood and it was very isolated.

The Most compassionate Buddha saw with His divine eye that Chatta Manavaka was going through the woods alone and that he was about to face a great danger.

Out of compassion for Chatta, the Supreme Buddha appeared in front of him.

Chatta Manavaka 02

Amazed, Chatta Manavaka recognized the Buddha. He felt very happy upon seeing the Fortunate One. The Buddha addressed Chatta Manavaka and spoke with him for a while.

By this time, Chatta Manavaka had not taken refuge in the Noble Triple Gem. He didn't even know about precepts.

So dear children, the Supreme Buddha, who has unmatched compassion for the whole world taught Chatta the value of the refuge in the Buddha, dhamma and sangha.

Chatta Manavaka was so intelligent. He understood the value of taking refuge in the Noble Triple Gem. He took refuge in the Supreme Buddha, the Noble Dhamma and the Noble Sangha wholeheartedly. Then the Buddha taught the precepts to Chatta Manavaka in this way;

- The first precept is:

    Pānāthipāthā Veramanī Sikkāpadaṅ Samādiyāmi.

    The meaning of that precept is 'I will not kill any living being.'

    Then he disciplined himself not to kill any living being.

- The second precept is:

    Adinnādānā Veramanī Sikkāpadaṅ Samādiyāmi.

    The meaning of that precept is: 'I will not steal one's belongings.'

    Then he disciplined himself not to steal.

Chatta Manavaka

- The third precept is:

    Kāmesu Michchāchārā Veramanī Sikkāpadaṅ Samādiyāmi.

    The meaning of that precept is: 'I will not engage in any sexual misconduct.'

    Then he disciplined himself not to engage in any sexual misconduct.

- The fourth precept is:

    Musāvādā Veramanī Sikkāpadaṅ Samādiyāmi.

    The meaning of that precept is: 'I will not lie and cheat others.'

    Then he disciplined himself not to lie and cheat others.

- The fifth precept is:

    Surāmeraya Majjapamādattāna Veramanī Sikkāpadaṅ Samādiyāmi.

    The meaning of that precept is: 'I will not use intoxicating drugs and liquor.'

    Then he disciplined himself not use intoxicating drugs and liquor.

So dear children, in this way, the Supreme Buddha taught about the Noble Triple Gem and the five precepts to Chatta Manavaka and established him in these five precepts.

Chatta Manavaka

Chatta Manavaka was so happy. He worshiped the Supreme Buddha with great respect. He took refuge of the Noble Triple Gem wholeheartedly. He observed the five precepts and vowed to protect them.

Thereafter, the Supreme Buddha taught the virtues of the Noble Triple Gem using three beautiful stanzas to Chatta Manavaka.

> **Yo Vadathaṅ Pavaro Manujesu**
> **Sakyamuni Bhagava Kathakichcho**
> **Pāragatho Balaviriya Samaṅgī**
> **Thaṅ Sugathaṅ Saranattamupemi**

> The Supreme Speaker amongst mankind,
> Sākyan Sage, O Holy One, whose task is done,
> Gone beyond, possessor of wisdom and courage;
> To thee, the Well-Gone One, I go for refuge.

The second verse is:

> **Rāga Virāga Maneja Masokaṅ**
> **Dhammamasaṅkatha Mappatikulaṅ**
> **Maduramimaṅ Pagunaṅ Suvibhattaṅ**
> **Dhammamimaṅ Saranattamupemi.**

Chatta Manavaka

The meaning of this stanza is:

Free from craving and sorrow-free,
Free from impurities is this Dhamma that never change,
Well proclaimed and highly practical,
To this very Dhamma I go for refuge.

The third stanza is:

**Yatta Cha Dinna Mahappalamāhu
Cathusu Suchīsu Purisayugesu
Attacha Puggala Dhammadasāthe
Sanghamimaṅ Saranattamupemi**

The meaning of this stanza is:

Making an offering greatly rewarding -
Noble Sangha, the followers of Dhamma
Eight in numbers, four in pairs;
To this Noble Sangha I go for refuge.

So dear children, the talented Chatta Manavaka learnt these stanzas at that very moment. Remembered them well and then continued his journey to his teacher's home through the woods.

Chatta Manavaka

But, Chatta Manavaka could go only a little distance. He was surrounded by a group of bandits. They hit Chatta Manavaka to get his belongings that he was taking to his teacher.

Chatta Manavaka died because of the beating. My dear children, even when Chatta Manavaka was being beaten mercilessly, he was only thinking about the qualities of the Supreme Buddha, the Noble Dhamma and the Noble Sangha. He was thinking about the precepts that he observed. He did not feel any anger or hatred towards the bandits.

Therefore, Chatta Manavaka was born as a Divine Prince in the happy world of Thāvatinsa. This Chatta Manavaka Divine Prince got a beautiful divine palace. He had many beautiful heavenly princes and princesses to attend to him.

Dear children, Chatta Manavaka got all these comforts simply because he took refuge in the Noble triple Gem and observed the five precepts for a very little period of time.

Chatta Manavaka

One day, Divine Prince Chatta Manavaka came to worship the Supreme Buddha and said:

"Oh, the Blessed One, I only got a moment to observe precepts and received such an abundant divine wealth. What a fortune those who protect the precepts all their lives will get!"

Now do you see my dear children the wealth one receives by observing precepts even for a moment and memorizing the virtues of the Noble Triple Gem?

So my dear children, it is of great value if you can learn these stanzas and memorize them. And observe the precepts from your childhood. Then your beautiful lives will continue to flourish, day by day your life will be more valuable.

- The end -

Mahamegha English Publications

Sutta Translations
Stories of Sakka, Lord of Gods: Sakka Saṁyutta
Stories of Great Gods: Brahma Saṁyutta
Stories of Heavenly Mansions: Vimānavatthu
Stories of Ghosts: Petavatthu
The Voice of Enlightened Monks: Theragāthā

Dhamma Books
The Wise Shall Realize

Children's Picture Books
The Life of the Buddha for Children
Chaththa Manawaka
Sumana the Novice Monk
Stingy Kosiya of Town Sakkara
Kisagothami
Kali the She-Devil
Ayuwaddana Kumaraya
Sumana the Florist
Sirigutta and Garahadinna
The Banker Anāthapiṇḍika

To order, go to www.mahamevnawa.lk

www.ingramcontent.com/pod-product-compliance
Lightning Source LLC
Chambersburg PA
CBHW041235040426
42444CB00002B/169